Lerner SPORTS™

SPAIN NATIONAL SOCCER TEAMS

ULTIMATE FAN GUIDE

JANIE SCHEFFER

Lerner Publications ◆ Minneapolis

To Dad and Katie—you will always be my Pelé and Mia Hamm.

Lerner Publications Company
An imprint of Lerner Publishing Group, Inc.
241 First Avenue North
Minneapolis, MN 55401 USA

For reading levels and more information, look up this title at www.lernerbooks.com.

Main body text set in Aptifer Slab LT Pro. Typeface provided by Linotype AG.

Editor: Matt Doeden **Designer:** Viet Chu **Photo Editor:** Lucien Brinkley
Lerner team: Sue Marquis

Library of Congress Cataloging-in-Publication Data

Names: Scheffer, Janie, 1992– author
Title: Spain national soccer teams : ultimate fan guide / Janie Scheffer.
Description: Minneapolis : Lerner Publications, [2026] | Series: Lerner Sports. World Cup fan guides | Includes bibliographical references and index. | Audience: Ages 7–11 | Audience: Grades 4–6 | Summary: "Few countries take their soccer more seriously than Spain. Find out how Spain's national team became a global powerhouse and learn about the game-changing styles and players that made it happen"— Provided by publisher.
Identifiers: LCCN 2025015081 (print) | LCCN 2025015082 (ebook) | ISBN 9798765689387 lib. bdg. | ISBN 9798348029302 pbk | ISBN 9798765698624 epub
Subjects: LCSH: Roja (Soccer team)—Juvenile literature | European Championship (Soccer tournament) | World Cup (Soccer) | Soccer fans—Spain—Juvenile literature | Soccer—Spain—History—Juvenile literature
Classification: LCC GV943.6.R54 S45 2026 (print) | LCC GV943.6.R54 (ebook) | DDC 796.334/660946—dc23/eng/20250813

LC record available at https://lccn.loc.gov/2025015081
LC ebook record available at https://lccn.loc.gov/2025015082

Manufactured in the United States of America
1-1012736-54806-8/7/2025

TABLE OF CONTENTS

Spain's fans pack the stadium at the 2024 Euro.

INTRODUCTION

2024 EURO CHAMPS

The crowd was on its feet late in the second half of the 2024 Men's European Championship (Euro) final. Spain and England were locked in a 1–1 tie. With regulation time running out, Spain moved the ball down the field once more to try to get a shot on net.

Spain's defender Marc Cucurella passed the ball to his teammate, forward Mikel Oyarzabal. Oyarzabal had broken ahead of his defender and was inside the box near the goal. He stretched his right foot as he slid, knocking the ball past the goalkeeper and into the net. Goal!

Five minutes later, the final whistle blew. Spain's fans and players celebrated the 2–1 victory. They were the Euro 2024 champs!

Men's and women's national soccer teams are made up of the most talented players from each country. For both men's and women's teams, the top title to earn is the World Cup. FIFA holds the World Cup tournament in

FAST FACTS

Spain's men's team defeated the Netherlands to win the World Cup in 2010.

Spain's women's team won the World Cup in 2023 after defeating England.

The men's team has won the most Euro titles. They won in 1964, 2008, 2012, and 2024.

In 2024, the women's team finished fourth in its first Olympic Games.

Forward Mikel Oyarzabal (*right*) scores the game-winning goal to give Spain the 2024 Euro championship.

a different country every four years. Beyond the World Cup, many national teams also compete in the Summer Olympics, which also occurs every four years.

On a local level, men's and women's national teams from Europe play in the Euro tournament every four years. Spain's players always work hard to win. Their fans are festive and loyal.

Spain's players celebrate their Euro title.

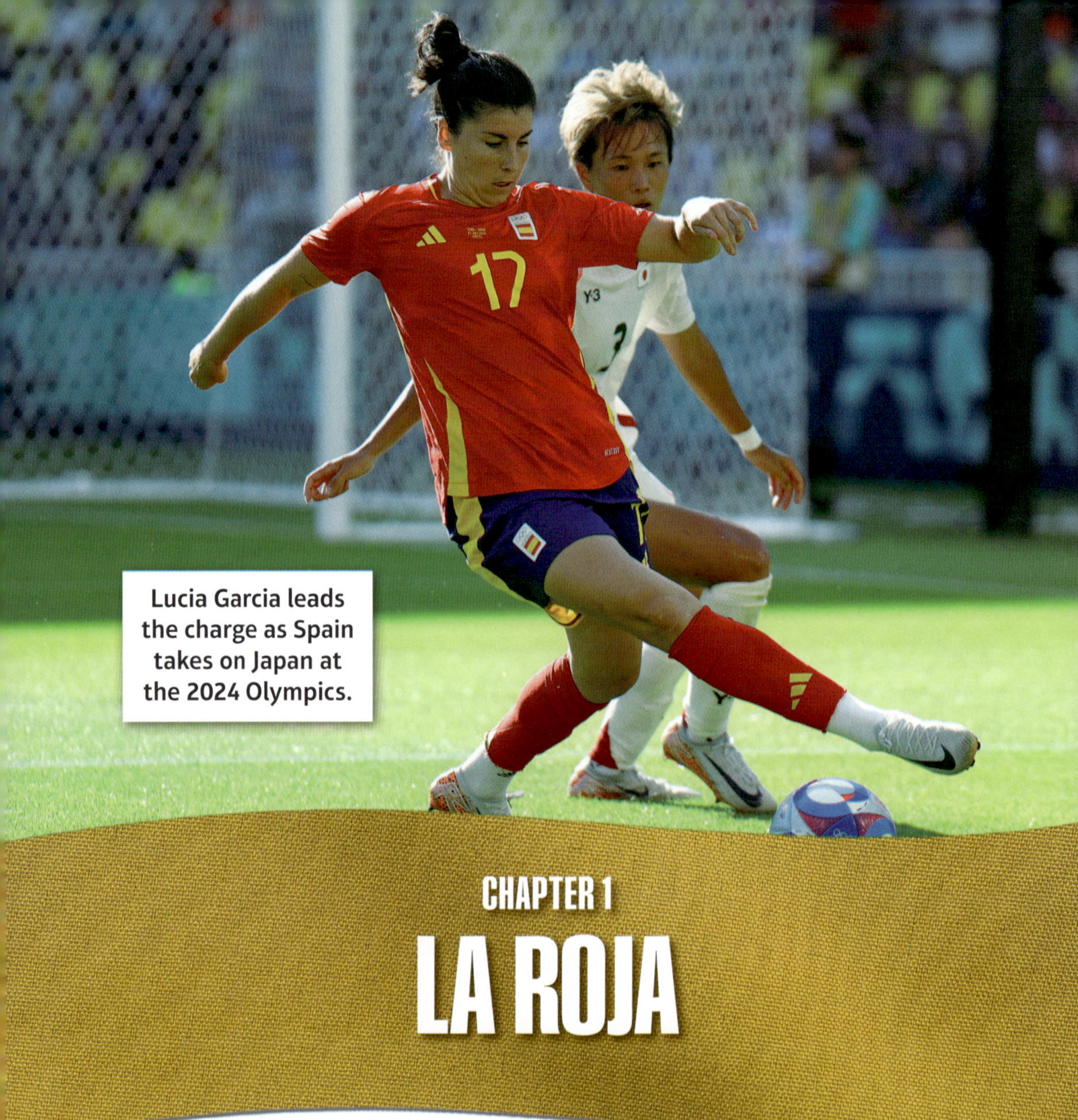

Lucia Garcia leads the charge as Spain takes on Japan at the 2024 Olympics.

CHAPTER 1

LA ROJA

The men's and women's soccer teams are known as La Roja, or the Reds. The men's team played its first official match in the 1920 Summer Olympics. It took more than a decade before La Roja became a contender in major soccer tournaments.

Spain placed fifth in their first World Cup in 1934, getting knocked out of a quarterfinal match by Italy. From their first World Cup, La Roja continued to get stronger. The team lifted its first major trophy in 1964 after winning the Euro. A fantastic midfielder and veteran player at the time, Luis Suarez, helped Spain secure the title.

Spain's players lift their coach, Jose Villalonga (*top right*), after their 1964 European Nations Cup championship.

Spain's women's team began playing in 1983. Two years later, the team tried to qualify for the 1987 Euro. But they failed to win a match. It would take years before the country embraced and respected women for playing the sport. For more than a decade, the team struggled with little success.

Spain players celebrate a goal against South Korea in the 2015 World Cup.

Spain's Mikel Lasa leaps for the ball in a 1992 Olympics match against Poland.

Spain's men had home field advantage at the 1992 Olympics in Barcelona. The team won the gold medal when captain Pep Guardiola led his teammates to victory against Poland. The early 2000s began a winning streak for La Roja. It included 35 straight wins between 2006 and 2009. The team's run to win the 2008 Euro title was part of the streak.

Men's coach Luis Aragones played a big part in Spain's success, and in the launch of the greatest period in the team's history. Aragones introduced a style of play called tiki-taka. The strategy kept the ball at the feet of a Spanish player by connecting many short passes. The ball moved quickly while Spanish players changed positions.

Luis Aragones lifts the trophy after Spain's 2008 Euro championship.

Spain (*in red and blue*) shows off its tiki-taka style at the 2010 World Cup.

The constant movement wore down opponents and led to many scoring chances. In a 2011 match, Spain passed the ball more than 40 times before scoring a goal! Spain's dominance also led to a 2010 World Cup title and the 2012 Euro title.

Until recently, many Spanish sports fans did not embrace women's soccer. With a growing youth program and recent success from the women's national team, there has been a shift in that attitude. Women's soccer—especially the national team—is booming.

Vicky Losada (*right*) lunges for the ball in the 2015 World Cup.

The breakthrough for women's soccer came in 2015 when Spain's women's team qualified for the World Cup for the first time. It was the start of the women's steady climb to becoming true contenders. Four years later, La Roja qualified again for the World Cup. This time, they advanced to the knockout round before losing to the United States 2–1.

Success kept coming. In 2021, Spain's women's team earned a spot in FIFA's top 10 world rankings. The women went on to win their first World Cup title in 2023 under the leadership of team captain Olga Carmona. In 2024, Spain won the UEFA Women's Nations League. They also finished fourth at the Olympics.

Spain celebrates after Irene Paredes scores a goal in a match against Colombia.

TV SUPERSTARS

There was no doubt in 2023 that Spain's women's team had captured the hearts of local fans. Almost six million Spanish viewers watched the final World Cup match.

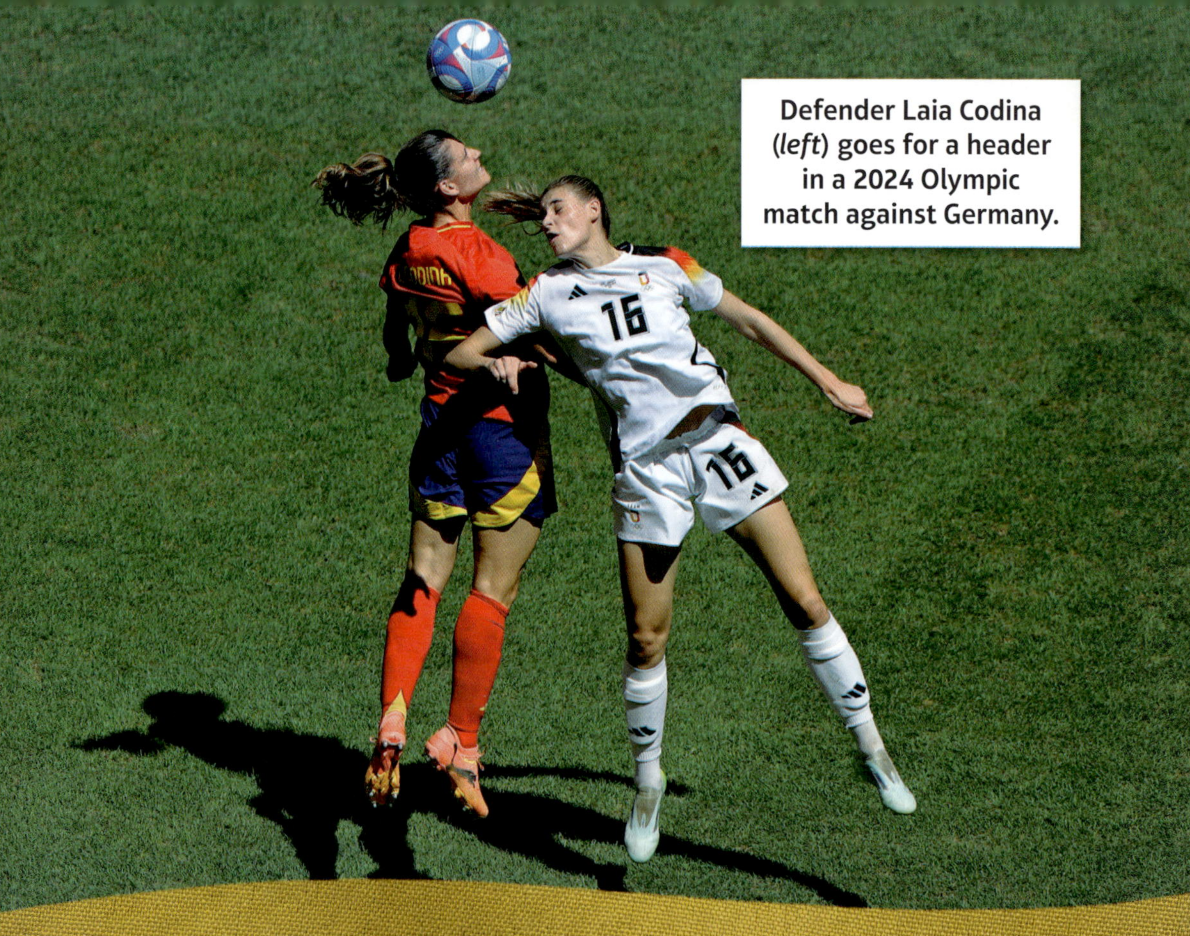

Defender Laia Codina (*left*) goes for a header in a 2024 Olympic match against Germany.

CHAPTER 2

WORLD CUP CHAMPS

Both of Spain's national teams have won a World Cup title. The men's team won its first and only World Cup in 2010, beating the Netherlands in extra time. Captain and goalkeeper Iker Casillas led the team's brilliant play. Spain battled the Netherlands for 90 minutes. At the end of regulation time, the score was tied 0–0. But Spain's midfield was made up of tiki-taka masters such as Andres Iniesta, Sergio Busquets, and Xavi Hernandez.

With four minutes left in extra time, La Roja put pressure on the Netherlands defense right outside the box. Cesc Fabregas made a pass to Iniesta inside the box. Iniesta struck with his right foot and beat the goalkeeper. It was the only goal of the match. The celebration was on for Spain's first World Cup title.

Andres Iniesta (*right*) scores the game-winning goal against the Netherlands in the 2010 World Cup final.

The Spanish men have not won another World Cup. But the team has lifted the Euro trophy four times. Two years before their World Cup title, Spain defeated Germany 1–0 to win the 2008 Euro title. With their top-scoring David Villa out due to injury, La Roja depended on other tiki-taka superstars.

Xavi Hernandez (*left*) challenges a German attacker in the 2008 Euro final.

Fernando Torres leaps over the German goalkeeper during the 2008 Euro final.

In the 33rd minute of the first half, Xavi Hernandez served up the ball to Fernando Torres. Torres broke through Germany's defense to shoot the ball past the goalkeeper. La Roja's lone goal clinched the title.

Spain's women's team won their first World Cup in 2023. This was a huge feat. Spain had not made it past the quarterfinal round in previous World Cups.

Midfielder Aitana Bonmati and forward Jenni Hermoso were two of the top goal scorers for the team. Bonmati

Aitana Bonmati winds up for a kick at the 2023 World Cup final.

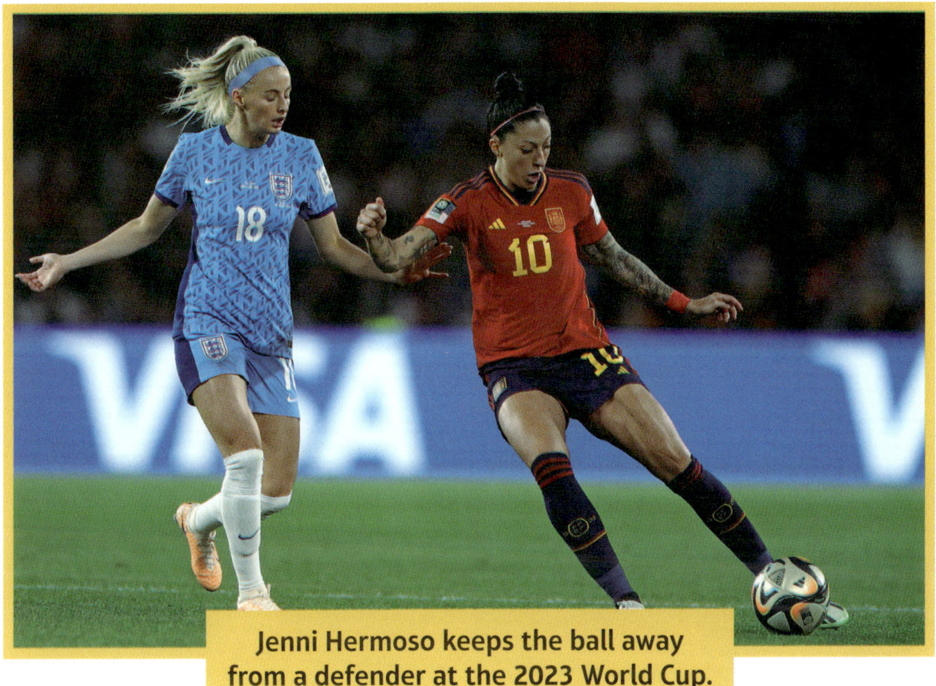

Jenni Hermoso keeps the ball away from a defender at the 2023 World Cup.

went on to win Player of the Tournament and the Golden Boot, while Hermoso won the Silver Boot. The Golden Boot is given to the top scorer of the World Cup tournament. The Silver Boot goes to the runner-up.

GOLDEN GLOVE

Spain's Iker Casillas won the Golden Glove award in 2010 for being the best goalkeeper at the World Cup. He only gave up two goals during the tournament.

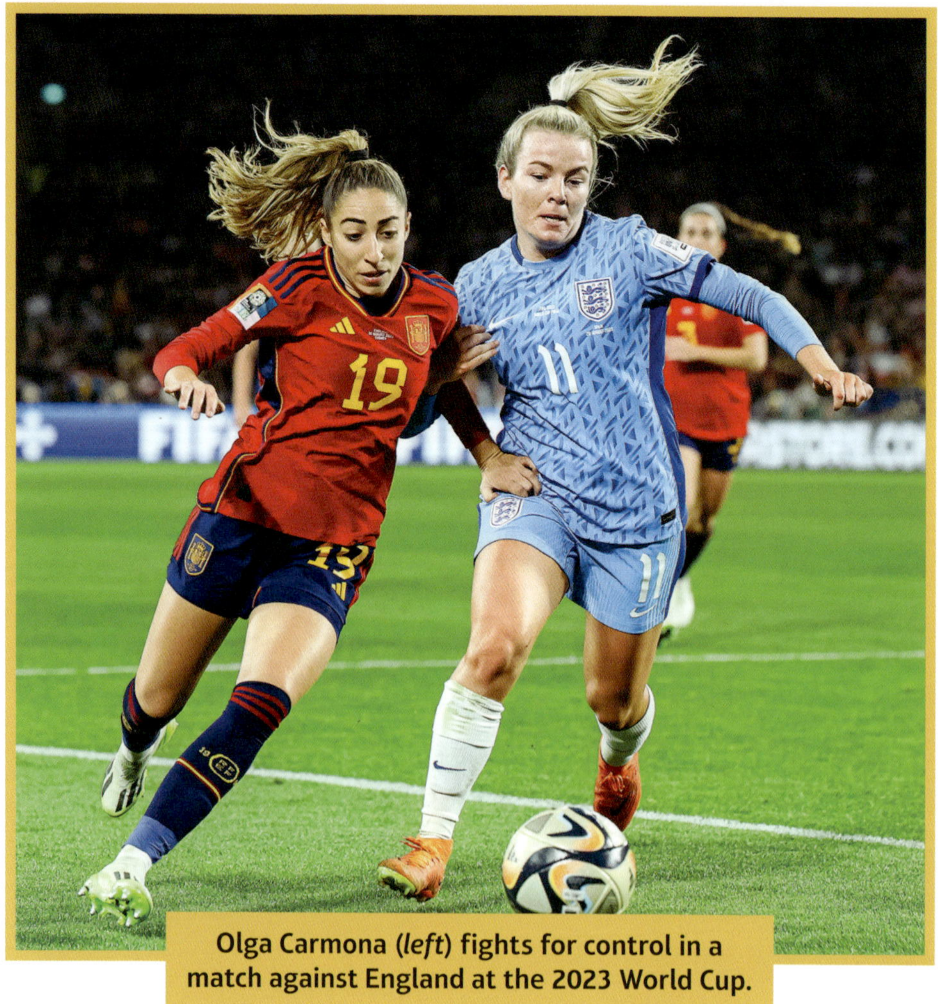

Olga Carmona (*left*) fights for control in a match against England at the 2023 World Cup.

In the final, against England, La Roja played its classic game strategy: controlling the ball. At about the 30-minute mark, Mariona Caldentey made a pass to Olga Carmona. Carmona struck the ball low, past England's goalkeeper, and just inside the goalpost. The lone goal held up, and Spain was the champion.

In the 2024 Euro, Spain's men earned their way to the final against England. The young, talented team used a strong passing game to wear down opponents. La Roja became four-time Euro champions. No other team has won the trophy that many times.

Mikel Oyarzabal (*right*) celebrates a goal with teammate Nico Williams at the 2024 Euro final.

The Spanish women played in their first Olympics in 2024. They came in ranked number one in the world but suffered a surprising loss to Brazil. In the bronze medal match, team captain Alexia Putellas stepped up to take a penalty kick to tie the game. Putellas took her shot, but Germany's goalkeeper stopped it. La Roja finished in fourth place.

Oihane Hernandez hits a header in the bronze-medal game at the 2024 Olympics.

Fans display Spanish flags in support of their team at the 2024 Olympics.

CHAPTER 3

FESTIVE FAN BASE

Soccer—called football in most of the world—is the most popular sport in Spain and a big part of the country's culture. Both national teams have a passionate fan base. If one of the national teams is playing, there are parties happening throughout the country. Groups of people gather in homes or public places to watch the matches. If it's a very important match, huge television screens are set up in city centers for viewing.

What happens before kickoff is a big part of the soccer experience for fans. They gather to eat, listen to music, and discuss the upcoming game before heading to the stadium. If it's a home match, they flock to the stadium long before the start.

Matches begin with Spain's national anthem, called "Marcha Real." Fans wear jerseys, wave flags, sing songs, and chant. It's a festive scene. During a game, fans feast on large bocadillos, or sandwiches, while cheering on their team.

Sandwiches are one of the foods Spanish fans enjoy during matches.

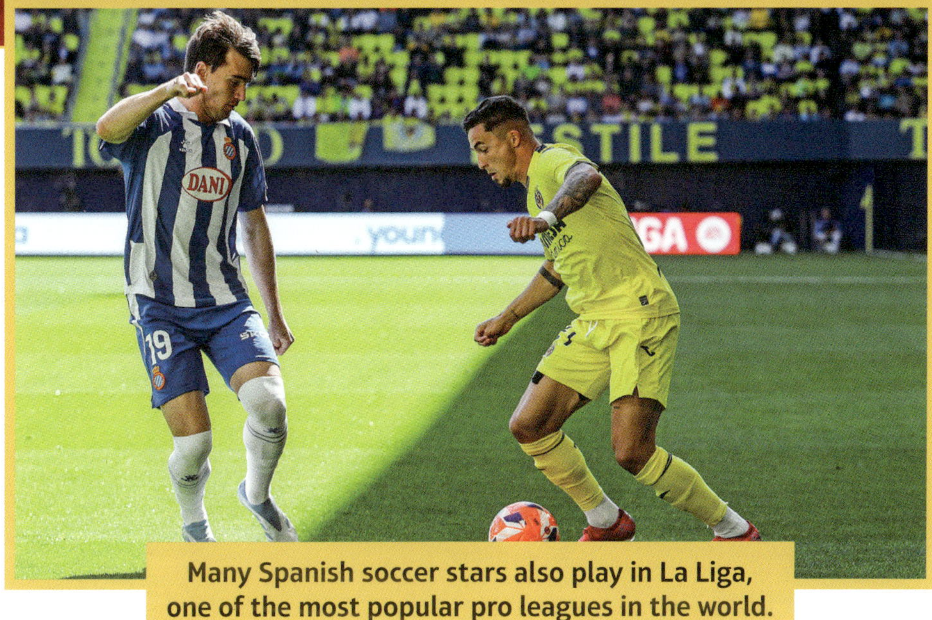

Many Spanish soccer stars also play in La Liga, one of the most popular pro leagues in the world.

Soccer fans in Spain are hopeful both teams can continue their success. The men are preparing for the 2026 World Cup. Meanwhile, women's soccer has boomed in Spain. This is an exciting time for the country, especially as the women's team gets ready for the 2027 World Cup. Fans can't wait to see what's next in Spain's long history of soccer success.

SPAIN'S PRO LEAGUES

Spanish fans love their pro teams. La Liga is Spain's pro men's soccer league. In 2022, Spain started Liga F, a women's pro league.

SPAIN MEN'S SOCCER TIMELINE

1920 Spain's men's team plays its first official match in the Summer Olympics.

1934 In their first World Cup, Spain finishes fifth.

1964 Spain wins its first Euro title.

1992 The team wins its first Olympic gold medal.

2008 Spain wins its second Euro title.

2010 The team wins its first World Cup title.

2012 Spain wins its third Euro title.

2024 The team wins its fourth Euro title.

SPAIN WOMEN'S SOCCER TIMELINE

1983 Spain's women's national team is formed.

1985 The team fails to qualify for the 1987 Euro.

2015 Spain qualifies for the World Cup for the first time.

2019 The team qualifies for the World Cup.

2021 The team reaches FIFA's top 10 ranking for the first time.

2023 Spain wins its first World Cup.

2024 The team plays in its first Olympic Games.

Spain wins the first UEFA Women's Nations League title.

GLOSSARY

box: the penalty area in front of each goal

captain: a player who is the official leader of a team

defender: a player who tries to stop the other team from scoring

extra time: time added to the end of a soccer game

FIFA: a group that oversees soccer around the world

midfielder: a soccer player whose main jobs are to pass the ball and defend

penalty kick: a free kick at the goal allowed for certain fouls or to decide the winner of some games

quarterfinal: the round of a tournament to determine the final four teams

regulation time: the standard length of a game before extra time. In soccer, regulation time is 90 minutes.

tiki-taka: a style of soccer developed in Spain that features frequent passing

LEARN MORE

Allen, Jules. *Portugal vs. Spain*. Spark, 2023.

Doeden, Matt. *G.O.A.T. Soccer Teams*. Lerner Publications, 2021.

Kiddle: Football Facts for Kids
https://kids.kiddle.co/Football

Kiddle: Spain National Football Team Facts for Kids
https://kids.kiddle.co/Spain_national_football_team

Shaw, Gina. *What Is the Women's World Cup?* Penguin Workshop, 2023.

Sports Illustrated Kids: Soccer
https://www.sikids.com/tag/soccer

INDEX

PHOTO ACKNOWLEDGMENTS

Image credits: Eurasia Sport Images/Just Pictures/Sipa USA via AP Images, p. 4; Ian MacNicol/Getty Images, p. 6; Marcio Machado/Eurasia Sport Images/Just Pictures/Sipa USA via AP Images, p. 7; Eddie Keogh - FIFA/FIFA via Getty Images, p. 8; Central Press/Hulton Archive/Getty Images, p. 9; Icon Sportswire via AP Images, p. 10; AP Photo/Thomas Kienzle, p. 11; AP Photo/Bernat Armangue, p. 12; jit bag/Wikimedia Commons (CC BY 2.0), p. 13; Matthew Lewis - FIFA/FIFA via Getty Images, p. 14; Icon Sport/Icon Sport via Getty Images, p. 15; Matt McNulty - FIFA/FIFA via Getty Images, p. 16; Clive Rose/Getty Images, p. 17; Alex Livesey/Getty Images, p. 18; AP Photo/Michael Probst, p. 19; Jose Breton/Pics Action/NurPhoto via Getty Images, p. 20; Maddie Meyer - FIFA/FIFA via Getty Images, p. 21; James Whitehead/Eurasia Sport Images/Getty Images, p. 22; Dan Mullan/Getty Images, p. 23; Marcus Brandt/picture-alliance/dpa/AP Images, p. 24; Ane Frosaker/SPP/Sipa USA via AP Images, p. 25; WHPics/Getty Images, p. 26; Ivan Terron/Europa Press via Getty Images, p. 27. Design elements: Ralf Hiemisch/Getty Images; Rifqyhsn Design/Getty Images; cunfek/Getty Images; poo worawit/Getty Images.

Cover: PETTER ARVIDSON/Bildbyran/Sipa USA via AP Images; Jose Manuel Alvarez Rey/JAR Sport Images/NurPhoto via AP.